Feathered Ones and Furry

By the Author

Feathered Ones and Furry

By Aileen Fisher
Illustrated by Eric Carle

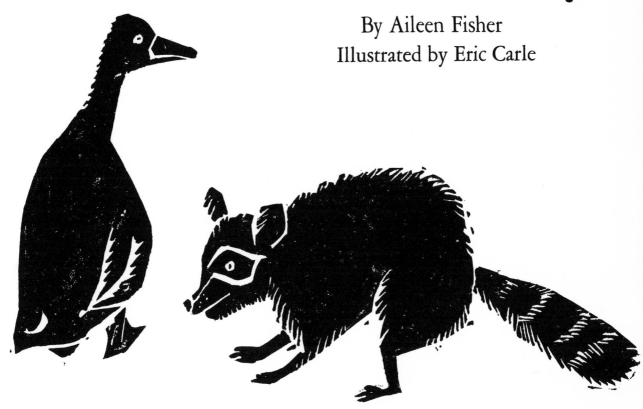

Thomas Y. Crowell Company, New York

More than half the verses in this book are new. Some are reprinted from *The Coffee-Pot Face, Inside a Little House,* and *That's Why,* copyright 1933 (renewed 1960), 1938 (renewed 1965), and 1946 by Aileen Fisher. "The Outdoor Christmas Tree" was originally published in *Story Parade,* copyright 1952 by Aileen Fisher. "Winter Surprise" was first published in *Highlights for Children,* copyright © 1965 by Highlights for Children, Inc., Columbus, Ohio. The following poems were first published in *My Weekly Reader:* "A Robin," "Bird Gardens," "Buried Treasure," "Chipmunk," "Drippy Weather," "Footprints," "In Fall," "Rabbit in the Grass," "Waiting," "New Puppy," "Off for a Hike," "Sniffing," "Who?," and "Winter Birds" copyright © 1962, 1963, 1964, 1965, 1966, 1967, 1969, 1970, by Xerox Corporation, and used by permission of American Education Publications/A Xerox Company, publisher of *My Weekly Reader.* "Winter Nests" is also used through the courtesy of *My Weekly Reader.*

L.C. Card 70-101925
ISBN 0-690-29451-4
      0-690-29452-2 (LB)
1 2 3 4 5 6 7 8 9 10

Bro-dart

1/76

4480

Contents

To Tinker and Terry

The Furry Ones

I like
the furry ones—
the waggy ones
the purry ones
the hoppy ones
that hurry,

The glossy ones
the saucy ones
the sleepy ones
the leapy ones
the mousy ones
that scurry,

The snuggly ones
the hug-ly ones
the never, never
ugly ones . . .
all soft
and warm
and furry.

I Like Them Feathery, Too.

I like them feathery, too—
I certainly, certainly do:
canary yellow
and lovebird green
and magpie black
with a shimmery sheen,
and fluttery bluebird blue.

I like them patterned
or feathery plain
from a tilt-tailed wren
to a long-legged crane.

But I like them best
for the news they bring
when you see the flash
of a feathery wing
at the end of winter,
and hear one sing,
so all of a sudden
you know it's SPRING.

I

How?

I

How do they know—
the sparrows and larks—
when it's time to return
to the meadows and parks?

How do they know
when fall is still here
it's the "thing" to go south
that time of the year?

Do you think that a bird
is just smart, or, instead,
that he carries a calendar
'round in his head?

II

How do they know—
the hornets and bees—
what direction to take
through the woods and the trees,

How far they should go,
how long they should roam,
and which way to turn
when it's time to go home?

Do you think that a bee
knows north from northwest—
or has he a compass
tucked under his vest?

Sniffing

Sniff, sniff, sniff,
my beagle goes
if it's calm
or if it blows,
getting newscasts
with his nose.

Sniff, sniff, sniff,
he pokes around
where his kind
of news is found
in the air
and on the ground.

Sniff, sniff, sniff . . .
I'm sniffing, too,
smelling news
that's coming through:
It's SPRING! . . . all warm
and fresh and new.

The Wrens

The wrens who rent our birdhouse
come back before it's May.

They hang their hats inside the door
and settle down to stay.

We never have to send a bill,
so punctual are they . . .

They start each morning, loud and clear,
to sing the rent away.

Drippy Weather

Geese keep dry
in drippy weather,
oiling feather after feather.

I keep just as dry
. . . and quicker.
I just have to wear my slicker.

Gosling

A gosling has a pleasant face—
a fuzzy head and cheek,
a black and round and snappy eye
and very smile-y beak.

What's for Rabbits?

"What's for rabbits
with nibbly habits?"
I asked one day in May.

  "Grass," said Father.
  "No fuss, no bother.
  No crumbs to brush away."

"What's for browsers
in soft fur trousers?"
I asked one day in June.

  "Weeds," said Mother.
  "One kind or other.
  No plate, no cup, no spoon."

"No table-setting!
No dinner-getting!
No plates to put away!
I wish *our* habits
were more like rabbits',"
I said, "from June to May!"

Rabbit in the Grass

You hardly show at all,
rabbit big, rabbit small,
by the bush near the wall
where the cloud-shadows sprawl.

You're part of the hill,
rabbit Jack, rabbit Jill,
where the grass-shadows spill . . .
if you just stay still.

Spring Morning

The sun was golden-shiny,
the trees were green and brown,
through windows very tiny
a little bird looked down.

He teetered on his leafy porch
upon a shady limb
and said "Hello" (I think he did)
and I said "Hi" to him.

A Badger

I'd like
to play with a badger.

Probably so would you.

He's very
clever at leapfrog
and somersaulting, too.

He likes
to play king-of-the-castle
at twilight on a stump:

We could try
to dethrone each other,
and tug, and shove, and jump.

We could shuffle-dance
in the meadow
when stars began to show . . .

But where's
there a badger to play with?
is what
I'd like to know.

A Kitten

"A kitten, a black one,
is all I want," I said.
Mother looked at Father
and sort of shook her head.
"Of course, I'd take a pony.
I'd take a cow or pig,
a billy goat, a nanny goat,
and several not so big.
"I'd take a hen and rooster,
a turkey that could strut;
I'd even take a CROCODILE . . ."
But Mother said, "Tut, tut—
"Goats may have their good points,
pigs, and roosters, too,
but don't you think a little cat,
a blackish one, would do?"

Pat-Cat

I had
a cat.

I named
him Pat.

But pret-
ty soon

It turned
out that

he was a different
kind of cat.
And now
that I've

Got kit-
tens (five!)

I'll let
them grow

Until I
KNOW . . .

and name them
sometime after that!

Cat Bath

After she eats,
my purry friend
washes herself
from end to end,

Washes her face,
her ears, her paws,
washes the pink
between her claws.

I watch, and think
it's better by far
to splash in a tub
with soap in a bar

And washcloth in hand
and towel on the rung
than have to do all
that work *by tongue.*

My Kitten

My kitten
has the softest fur,
as soft as silk to touch.
I smoothe her,
and she starts to purr:
"Thank you very much."

And even
when I'm doing things
or when I want to play
she smoothes herself
on me and sings:
"Thank you, anyway."

Cows

When I look at cows and think
how they stretch their necks to drink,
how they stretch their necks to graze
in different places different days,
I'm thankful I don't have to kink
MY poor neck so many ways.

Horses

Standing up for sleeping
the way they do,
horses must be just as tired
after sleeping's through.

A Horse to Ride

Sometimes a horse
has a rumpled hide,
or a sway in his back,
or his back's too wide
for my sort of legs
to sit astride,

But I wouldn't care
how he looked *outside*
if I only, only, only
had a horse to ride.

A Pony

Wish I had a pony
who would nuzzle, nuzzle, nuzzle
with his silky-satin muzzle.

Wish I had a pony
I could straddle, straddle, straddle,
so I wouldn't need a saddle.

Wish I had a white one,
a just-the-proper-height one.

Wish I had a red one,
a star-upon-his-head one.

Wish I had a brown one,
a trotting-up-and-down one.

Wish I had a pony
with a name like Tuck or Tony
who was plump instead of bony
(though a bony one would do) . . .

Wish it didn't take so long
for wishes to come true.

Tails

"Squirrels are lucky that they wear
tails," said John, "of bushy hair:

"When they leap, it seldom fails,
they stay balanced by their tails.

"And at night," said John, "they use
tails for blankets when they snooze.

"So the squirrels are lucky TWICE
they aren't made with tails-like-mice."

Funny Old Moles

All I can say is that busy old moles
are funny old moles indeed:
they burrow so hard in their tunnel-y holes
they never have time to read,
they never have time to roller skate,
or coast down a hill like me—
they only can dig at a furious rate
to find little grubs for tea;
and the more they burrow, the more they eat,
for the more-to-eat they need!
Which is why I say that busy old moles
are funny old moles indeed.

Squirrel

Outside my window
is a tree
that *seems*
to be the property
of someone small
with bright black eyes
and tail terrific
for his size.

He scampers up
and scampers down
our tree of green
and gold and brown,
and never pays
us rent, but we
pay peanuts
for his company.

Who?

Who lives inside a house
that doesn't have a door?

It doesn't have a window
or light inside, what's more.

Who lives inside a house
with walls so frail and thin
that when he once comes out
he cannot go back in?

I'd Not Be a Robin

Although I'd be pretty
and dressed very neat,

Although I could twitter
and chirrup and tweet,

I'd not be a robin
with hoppity feet—

I never could swallow
what I'd have to eat!

A Robin

I wonder how
a robin hears?

I never yet
have seen his ears.

But I have seen him
cock his head,

And pull a worm
right out of bed.

The Sparrow

I found a speckled sparrow
between the showers of rain.

He thought the window wasn't there
and flew against the pane.

I picked him up and held him.
He didn't stir at all.

I hardly felt him in my hand,
he was so soft and small.

I held him like a flower
upon my open palm.

I saw an eyelid quiver,
though he lay still and calm.

And then . . . before I knew it
I stood alone, aghast:

I never thought a bird so limp
could fly away so fast!

Bird Gardens

If birds had gardens,
what would they grow?

Not carrots or beets
or beans in a row,

But weeds, weeds, weeds
to make seeds, seeds, seeds

For birds to eat
in the cold and snow.

A Duck

With legs so short and far apart,
a duck just doesn't have the art
of stepping out and looking smart.

But when he slips into the pond
(a place of which he's very fond)
and skims into the blue beyond,

He swims so fast and far and fine
in such a smooth unsplashy line
I'd almost trade his legs for mine.

The Hawk

Instead of using his wings to fly
the hawk just waits on a hill of sky
till a frisky wind that blows from town
swishes him up and swoops him down.

Instead of using a pine or birch
he makes a frollicking wind his perch,
and tilts his wings till away he glides
to the roof of the sky and down its sides.

Wish *I* knew how to get such rides!

Like a Summer Bird

How would it be
to fly and fly
like a summer bird
in the rain-washed sky
after the sun
had ironed it dry?

How would it be
to sleep in a tree
on a rocking-chair branch
when the wind blew free,
with a sound in your ears
like the sound of the sea?

How would it *be*?

Sandpipers

I like to see the teetertails
run out of reach
when wave-fingers stretch
up the wet shiny beach.

I like to see the teetertails
race back in glee
when the fingers draw back
to the hands of the sea.

The Pelican

What does the pelican
have for dinner?
   Fish.
What makes the pelican
get no thinner?
   Fish.
What does the pelican
have for supper?
   Fish.
And when he's an early
getter-upper?
   Fish.

What does the pelican
have to munch
for breakfast
and dinner
and tea and brunch
and parties
and picnics
and snacks and lunch?
   Fish!

Isn't it good
the pelican finds
fish in the sea
of *different kinds?*

Fish, fish, fish.

At the Zoo

I like the zebra
   at the zoo,
his stripes are more
   than just a few.
I like the stripes
   on tigers, too,
and springboards
   on a kangaroo.

I like the furry
   black old bear,
and camel dressed
   in camel's hair,
and monkeys
   swinging in the air . . .
but I am glad
   I'm not so rare

Or I might be
   included, too,
among the creatures
   in the zoo.

Pines

Pines on the hill
go swashy-swish
when autumn is here
and it's windy-ish.

Swashy-swish
go the pines in fall—
the big, the middle-
sized ones, and small.

And the more it blows
the louder they get,
till jays can't hear
themselves think, I bet.

Looking for Feathers

I like to look for feathers
on a late-in-summer walk,
feathers in the brambles
or caught upon a stalk.

All the birds lose feathers
as summer starts to wane,
feathers brightly colored,
feathers sort of plain.

All the birds grow new ones—
some for flying away,
some for feather blankets
on a snowy day.

Feathers should be showing
in the weeds and grass . . .
I wonder why they always
are hiding when I pass?

Off for a Hike

My puppy can't speak English,
she doesn't know a letter,
but her wiggles and her wriggles
when she sees me get my sweater
and her raggle-taggle waggles
when I pack a lunch and pet her
are just as good as talking is . . .
and maybe even better.

After School

My puppy needs a brushing,
though he doesn't know what for,

And then he needs an outing,
and a tussle on the floor,

And then he needs his supper,
and a going-out once more,

And every day I wonder
what I used to do *before*.

New Puppy

I can't *wait*
for school to be over,
can't *wait*
to rush down the street,

For I
have a new brown puppy
with funny white socks
for feet.

He's the wiggliest
bundle of wiggles
you ever
could hope to see.

I can't *wait* . . .
and I hope my puppy
is waiting as hard
for me.

Weasel

Once we saw a weasel
in a rocky
sort of place.

His four short legs
were running
and he had a hurried face.

He probably was going
to his far-off
hidden den,

But we *always*
look for weasels
when we pass that place again.

In Fall

Which would you choose
to be in fall—
a chipmunk curled
in a cuddly ball
sleeping the cold away,

Or a deer mouse
searching the frosty weeds
to fill his cupboard
with nuts and seeds
for many a snowy day?

Chipmunk

Chipmunk,
chipmunk,
you're a skippety
skipmunk!

Flick,
flick,
over a stick,
under the bushes
thin and thick
you scamper along
so quickety quick

You ought
to be called
a quickmunk
instead of a
chippity chipmunk.

Winter Surprise

We filled a feeder for the birds
and said some very shoo-y words
to warn a squirrel upon a limb
the seeds and suet weren't for *him*.

We tied the feeder to a string
and to a bough, and let it swing.
"No squirrel can scamper down a cord,"
we said, and threw a nut reward.

The squirrel looked, and cocked his head,
and flicked his tail, and off he sped
to brace himself against the limb
and pull the feeder up to *him*!

Randy Raccoon

Randy Raccoon,
you prowl by the moon,
you prowl in the starlight, too.

While I am in bed
you're roving, instead,
the whole of a mild night through.

Randy Raccoon,
you're sleepy as soon
as weather brings snow and frost.

Then, cozy and warm,
through blizzard and storm,
you catch up on sleep you've lost.

First Snowfall

The little mouse
in her knothole house
where her bed
is warm and dry . . .

Does she get a shock
when it's snow-o'clock
and whiteness
fills the sky?

She only knows
about grass that grows
and weed-stalks
turned to gold.

She never has heard
a single word
about the snow
and cold.

On a sudden night
when the world turns white
and green and gold
are through,

The little mouse
in her knothole house . . .
does she wonder
what to do?

Winter Nests

Not all the nests are empty
with winter white and deep.

Inside the little wren house
a wasp has crawled to sleep.

The catbird nest is covered
with hay to make a house.

And do you know who lives there?
Mrs. Whitefoot Mouse.

Buried Treasure

How do squirrels remember
when woods are white with snow
where they hid the pine cones
they buried months ago?

Sometimes they remember,
and sometimes they do *not*.
Look at all the seedlings
from cones the squirrels forgot!

Off They Flew

I said some very coaxing words
and threw some bread crumbs to the birds,
but off they flew among the weeds
to hunt for dry old sunflower seeds.

Waiting

"Hurry!" say the voices
in the snowy trees.
"Hurry!" say the juncos
and the chickadees.

"Yesterday you fed us
and the day before.
Today it's just as chilly
and it's snowed some more.

"Hurry!" say the voices.
"How can you forget?
We're waiting for our breakfast
and the table isn't set!"

Winter Birds

I can't go visit a snowbird—
I don't know where he stays.

I can't go visit a chickadee—
he has such flitty ways.

I can't go visit a bluejay
atop a snowy tree,

And so I scatter seeds around
and have them visit *me*.

Back Again

Where they go in summer
my mother doesn't know,

But chickadees are back as soon
as wrens and bluebirds go,

And all the twitty juncos
the day it starts to snow

Come looking in our feeders.
I wonder how they *know*.

Rabbit Tracks

There's a crevice in the granite
   in the mountains where I live.
There's a rabbit in a burrow
   in the rocks, I'm positive.
Or maybe there are several
   hidden down between the cracks,
but all that ever shows of them
                are tracks
                      and tracks
                           and
                             tracks.

There's a snowdrift on the granite
   in the mountains where I stay,
but underneath in burrows
   it is warm and tucked away.
And though my puppy scratches
   and we peer in all the cracks,
the rabbits only let us see
            their tracks
                 and tracks
                     and
                       tracks.

Footprints

In summertime
it's hard to know
where dogs
and mice
and rabbits go:
Their grassy footprints
never show—
you can't tell where
they lead.

In wintertime
there's little doubt
where wild and tame ones
run about:
Their snowy footprints
write it out . . .
and I know how to read!

Merry Christmas

I saw on the snow
when I tried my skis
the track of a mouse
beside some trees.

Before he tunneled
to reach his house
he wrote "Merry Christmas"
in white, in mouse.

The Sleepyheads

I feel sorry
for a bear
in cold and snowy weather.

He sleeps inside
a dark old lair
for weeks and months together.

And I feel sorry
for a skunk
(although that may sound funny),

Not stirring
from its winter bunk
when days are crisply sunny.

And woodchucks
sleep the cold away.
For months you never see them.

They're all asleep
on *Christmas Day,*
poor things . . .
I wouldn't be them!

The Outdoor Christmas Tree

Little winter cottontails,
where is it you stay?
Lest you have forgotten tales,
turn your ears this way:

    Do you know what day it is,
    now the world is white?
    Do you know what way it is
    to my house tonight?
    Little winter cottontails,
    come and see a sight!

Little hoppy cottontails
scrunching in the snow,
lest you have forgotten tales
of a year ago,
tilt your ears and listen now:

    We've a tree, alight!
    All its branches glisten now—
    oh, but it's a sight.
    Little hoppy cottontails,
    come and see tonight.

About the Author

Aileen Fisher lives in the midst of the natural beauty of which she writes with such knowledge and love. From her house at the foot of Flagstaff Mountain in Boulder, Colorado, she can easily reach trails leading into the woods and up the mountains where she can observe the many varieties of wild birds and animals with which the area abounds. Miss Fisher also has some "furry ones" at home: her dog, Terry, and her cat, Tinker, to whom this volume is affectionately dedicated.

Miss Fisher was born in the Upper Peninsula of Michigan. When she was five, her family moved to a farm near Iron River, and it was there that she learned to love the outdoors and to look forward to the changing seasons. Her first poetry was written for the high school column in the local newspaper. Since that time she has written many books and plays for children. She attended the University of Chicago and later received a degree in journalism from the University of Missouri.

About the Illustrator

Eric Carle, internationally known designer and illustrator, is also the creator of outstanding picture books for children that have been published in many countries around the world. He has been praised by *Graphis* magazine for his "warm grasp of the subject matter" in his highly original and brilliant posters and illustrations. This is most evident in the striking lino-cuts he has created for this book. Simple and graphically strong, they are also eloquently expressive of the artist's love for birds and animals—and for children. Mr. Carle has two children of his own, as well as two very furry cats and a pet iguana.

Eric Carle is the author and illustrator of *The Tiny Seed*, *Do You Want to Be My Friend?*, and several other books for the very youngest readers. One of his recent books was chosen by *The New York Times* as one of the ten best illustrated books of the year, and his *1, 2, 3 to the Zoo* was awarded first prize as the most outstanding picture book at the 1970 International Children's Book Fair in Bologna, Italy.

Born in the United States, Mr. Carle lived and studied for many years in Germany. He now divides his time between Vermont and New York City.